TO DAVID GROSSMAN

WRESTLING JERUSALEM

A PLAY
BY AARON DAVIDMAN

Contact: **info@wrestlingjerusalem.com**

ISBN: 1518648304
ISBN-13: 978-1518648304

WRESTLING JERUSALEM premiered at Intersection for the Arts in San Francisco, CA March 12 – April 6, 2014. It was performed by the author. The production was directed by Michael John Garcés. Scenic design was by Nephelie Andonyadis; Lighting design was by Allen Willner; Sound design and composition was by Bruno Louchouarn; Choreography was by Stacey Printz. The Stage Manager was Karen Runk.

The play was commissioned by Ari Roth, Artistic Director of Mosaic Theater of DC, and was developed in part by Theatre J, Sundance Institute Theatre Program, Traveling Jewish Theatre and Playwrights Foundation.

Upstage hangs an abstract painted backdrop: textures that suggest the layered landscape of the Middle East.

The stage is bare.

Music, sound and light are used to create the layers of time and space in which the action takes place.

There are no costume changes, rather, vocal inflection, dialect and physicality delineate change of character.

The play is performed without interruption by one actor.

Each of us is encased in an armor which we soon, out of familiarity, no longer notice. There are only moments which penetrate it and stir the soul to sensibility.

-- Martin Buber

Who is wise?
He who learns from all people.

--Pirkei Avot.

CHARACTERS:

AARON	Narrator. 40's.
TARIQ	Palestinian man. 40's.
NADAV	Israeli man. 50's.
FARAH	Palestinian woman. 30's.
ARIK	Israeli man. 50's.
JACOB	American man. 50's.
TALI	Israeli woman. 30's.
PROF. HOROWITZ	British man. 40's.
DR. TZIPORA	Israeli woman. 40's.
TAMAR	Israeli woman. 60's.
NADIA	Palestinian woman. 60's.
NABIL	Palestinian man. 50's.
DANIEL	American man. 20's.
AVRAM	Israeli man. 40's.
IBRAHIM	Palestinian man. 60's.
RABBI MOSES	American man. 60's.
AMIR	Israeli man. 20's.

1.

It's complicated.

You might say it all started in 1948
Which you might call *Al Nakbeh*
The Catastrophe
You might say it all started in 1948
Which you might call *Milchemet HaAtzma'ut*
The War of Independence

You might go back to World War I
Blame the British
Say they fucked up a thousand years of decent relations
Between Jews and Arabs

You might say it was the 1929 massacre of Jews in Hebron
You might say it was the 1994 massacre of Muslims in
Hebron
Or the 1982 massacre at Sabra and Shatila
Or the 2003 massacre at the Tel Aviv bus station

No, no, you might say,
It was 1967
The Six Day War
That's when the real problems started
No, you might say
It was the Yom Kippur War
1973, that was it

But really, you might say,
It was 1947
The Partition Plan
United Nations Resolution 181
The Arabs should have accepted 181
And they would have had a better deal
Than they're ever going to get now
But you might say
The UN never should have adopted Resolution 181

Because it was a European land grab
Look,
You might say
It was the invasion of Lebanon
It was the first Intifada
It was the second Intifada
It was the withdrawal from Gaza
It was the war in Gaza

No, no
It's the Settlements
Definitely the Settlements
No, it's the terror attacks
The bus bombs, the cafes
No, it's the wall and the check points
No, it's the tunnels from Egypt
and the missiles in S'derot
No, it's Iran
It's all about Iran

No, it's the politicians
It's all about the politicians
Golda blew it
Peres blew it
Arafat blew it
Barak blew it
Olmert blew it
Sharon blew it
Clinton blew it
Bush blew it
Obama is blowing it

If they just hadn't killed Rabin
If we just hadn't killed Rabin
If the Ultra Orthodox just didn't have so much political
power
If the Arab League would just do more
If the Media just wasn't so biased

If the Right Wing Christians would just stop funding
Settlements
If AIPAC would just be more critical of Israel
If J Street would just be less critical of Israel
If we just had a real partner on the other side
If Netanyahu would just...
If Abbas would just...
If the Palestinians would just lay down their arms
If the Israelis would just get out of the West Bank
If the world would just step up and get more involved
If the world would just back off and stay of out it

If, if, if, if, if, if
If!

2.
A rabbi walks into a bar.

Bartender says, "Nu, Rabbi, what can I get for you this
morning?" The rabbi says, "A *bisseleh* shnaps." Bartender
pours him a drink. Rabbi says, "You call that a *bissel*?"
"Rabbi, where've you been this morning?" "Oy. Where I go
every morning. To pray at the Western Wall." "How long
have you been praying in the morning at the Wall, Rabbi?"
"How long? Forty years. Every day for forty years I pray to
my God at the Western Wall." "Rabbi, what do you pray for
every day for forty years?" "What do I pray--? I pray that
there should be peace between the Jews and the Arabs.
That all the fighting should stop. And that our children
should grow in safety and friendship." "Rabbi, I'm
impressed by your dedication and commitment, but I have
to ask, after for 40 years of these prayers, how do you
feel?" "How do I feel? How do I feel? I FEEL LIKE I'M
TALKING TO A FUCKING WALL!"

3.
And my heart beats
I talk to a friend in Tel Aviv

My heart beats faster
I read the paper
My heart beats faster
I watch the news
My heart beats faster
I hear someone on the street
In a cafe
On the subway
They say the word *Israel*
And my heart beats faster
My breath grows short
Israel
Yisrael
The charge
Electric
A trigger
Physiology
Fight/Flight
They call it
The Hind Brain
Activated
Automated
Amped up

Not always
For me
Israel
The word
My father's name
Srolik, they called him
Short for *Yisrolik,* Yiddish
His first language
1930's
Brighton Beach, Brooklyn
Stick ball
Knishes
Yiddish *Shule*
Summer camp

Upstate New York
Pine trees
Jewish girls
Communists
Yiddish Culture
Labor
Workers rights
Women's rights
Civil rights
Paul Robeson
Woody Guthrie
Emma Lazarus
Harriet Tubman
Chana Senesh
Chaney, Goodman and Schwerner
All names of cabins at Camp Kinderland

I was a camper there too
I chased Jewish girls there too
I sang Yiddish songs there too

(sings)
O Kinderland du tsoyberland
Unter himlen frayen
Mir kumen zikh do opruen
Shtarken un banaiyen
O kinder kinder Kinderland
Far kinder a ganeydn
Mir shpiln zich, mir lernen zich
Mir lebn do in freydn

Equality
Freedom
Justice
For all
Jewish values
I was taught
By a man named Israel

Yisra-el
The one who wrestles with God

And here I am. *The People, United, Will Never Be Defeated.* A pro-peace rally. Flags. Banners. Bull horn blazing. *All Arabs are not terrorists!* Thousands moving across the plaza. Young women. Young men. *All Israelis are not oppressors!* The heat of bodies press together. Sun bright over head. *The people of Gaza want freedom!* Blue sky above, reaching out forever. *The people of Israel want peace!* Mouth dry. Elbow to elbow. The crowd thickens. *We want justice, we want peace.* Roar of voices. *We want justice, we want peace!* Roar. Behind me, first, it comes. *Free Free Palestine.* Flags. Fists. *Free Free Palestine!* Banners. Bodies press. *Free Free Palestine!!* A surge of words. A crackle of fire. It spreads. *End The Occupation.* Fists squeeze tight. *End The Occupation.* Fists fill the air. *Death To Israel.* What? What? *Death To Israel!* What? What?! A blur of faces. Fight/Flight. A fog of sound. Fight/Flight. *Death To The Jews! Death To The Jews! Death To The Jews!!*

4.

> Song. The BESHT Niggun.
> (A Chassidic melody without words)

The Kabbalists, the Jewish mystics, tell a story of creation. Once there were vessels of light that contained all that is good in the universe. But this goodness was so powerful that the vessels, with their thin shells, could not contain it. And the vessels burst. And the light of goodness was scattered. Sparks and shards of light flew into all the corners of the world. They're hidden amidst all of us. And it's the work of human beings, say the Kabbalists, to find those sparks, those fragments of goodness, and put them back together. It's how we heal the world, they say.

We gather the broken pieces of goodness and put them back together.

Song. Reprise of the BESHT Niggun,
which transforms into...

5.

(sings)
Allah hu akbar. Allah hu akbar.
Allah hu akbar. Allah hu akbar.
Ash-hadu an la ilahah ill allah.
Ash-hadu an la ilahah ill allah.
Ash-hadu anna Muħammadan rasulullah.
Ash-hadu anna Muħammadan rasulullah.

TARIQ: Excuse me, are you Muslim?
AARON: No. I'm...American.
TARIQ: Islam is the one true religion because it respects all religions.
AARON: I know.
TARIQ: You *are* Muslim?
AARON: No.
TARIQ: Muslims respect all the prophets: Abraham, Moses, Jesus, Muhammad. We don't worship Muhammad like Christians worship Jesus. We worship only Allah, the One God.
AARON: It's exactly the same for Jews.
TARIQ: You are Jewish?
AARON: *(Uncomfortable)*
TARIQ: We are all the same under God.
AARON: Then why do we keep killing each other?
TARIQ: This is the problem. What is your name?
AARON: Aaron.
TARIQ: *Haroun! Haroun, al-Rashid!* He was the most famous caliph of Bagdad. I am Tariq. Here is information about Islam. Come, have coffee with me.
AARON: I'm sorry. I have to catch a bus to Ramallah.
TARIQ: What is in Ramallah?
AARON: I'm trying to answer some questions.
TARIQ : What questions?
AARON: It's...complicated.

TARIQ: You have deep questions, *Haroun?*
AARON: I've got a few things on my mind.
TARIQ: Come with me, Haroun. Allah will answer all your questions.
AARON: Not today. Thank you.

I'm looking for the number 18 bus—

TARIQ: *Haroun,* you know Abraham, Moses, Jesus and Muhammad all are our prophets?
AARON: Yes. Of course.
TARIQ: Then *Haroun*, you are already a Muslim!

Who knew?

I'm looking for the number 18 bus in East Jerusalem, somewhere up the street from Damascus Gate, the Arab entrance to the Old City. I'm only a few blocks from the Jewish part of Jerusalem, but it feels like another world. The smells of the food vendors; the language in the air; the gestures of the people in the street. All so different. I can't find the bus stop and I have a nervous feeling of being...*on the other side.* I've been to Israel many times. I've never been to Ramallah.

When I finally find the small bus, I pay 6 sheckels and get on. I sit in the back. I'm sure I'm the only Jewish person on board. But I feel invisible. No one seems to notice to me. The atmosphere is quiet. Tired. As soon as we get on the highway the bus is stopped by the Israeli police.

ISRAELI OFFICER: Tad'zeut Vaksha.

I clutch my passport. I don't want to pass it forward. I just sit there. The officer doesn't see me? Now my invisibility feels conspicuous. There's a blank stare in the eyes of the middle-aged Palestinian men as they pass their ID cards forward. "Do you speak English?" A woman turns to me.

8

"Did they ask to see your ID? No. You see how they humiliate us."

Ten minutes later we approach the Kalandia check-point. There's a long line of cars and people on foot waiting to get through. Manned by the Israeli army, Kalandia is one of the few places to cross from Israel into the West Bank. And from the West Bank into Israel. Hundreds of kilometers of electric fences, barb-wire, trenches and 8 meter high concrete walls run North and South of this crossing, creating a de-facto border. B'Tselem, the Israeli Human Rights Organization, calls this structure the *Separation Barrier.* The Israelis call it the *Security Fence.* The Palestinians call it the *Apartheid Wall.*

Whatever you want to call it, it's massive. And intimidating. And haunting. The Kalandia crossing is a rocky no-man's land with two giant ominous watch-towers surrounded by fences laced with barbed wire.

Concentration camps. All I can think of is concentration camps. Concentration camps?! A life-time of Holocaust imagery comes lurching forward from the back of my mind. NO! Don't think of concentration camps, there's no moral equivalency here. It's not the same, it's not the same!

Guard towers, guard dogs, barb wire, soldiers, machine guns, refugees, suitcases. Now the Jews are the guards and I'm on the train going into the camp. And I--, I--, I--, I--, I--, I--, I--

I remember Nadav.

> NADAV: And the craziest thing, Aaron. When I got here—I did not yet know my Gili was on this bus. I did not know. I heard on the radio of the *piggua,* the bombing, and I come right here—it's my

neighborhood—in Haifa we don't expect such things. And I stood here in the street and I could smell burnt flesh in the air. And at that moment I had a strange feeling. I thought this must be the smell the people smelled coming off the trains in Auschwitz. The smell of the crematoriums. My parents were the only survivors of their families to make it out alive. Every other member of my family was killed. Every single one. Uncles, aunts, everyone completely destroyed. And here, 60 years later, My Gili, burned alive in such a brutal murder.

He was thirteen years old. He was in the peace camp for Palestinian and Israeli children just two weeks before! Look, I don't hate the Arabs. But build the wall, absolutely build the wall. Let them live over there. And we'll live over here. I'm finished!

And I'm staring at this wall out the window of the bus at the Kalandia check-point, and six million ghosts chase me as we drive through. And I wonder if they will ever rest.

The bus lurches and swerves as the driver tries to avoid an obstacle course of pot-holes in the road. We're clearly not in Israel any more. We pass by the bleak buildings of the Kalandia refuge camp and I have the unsettling feeling we've entered a giant outdoor prison.

Ten more minutes and we arrive in Ramallah. A bustling city. Huge billboards everywhere in Arabic. Traffic. People in the street. I get off the bus at the central station. I find the café. I'm looking for Farah. A woman in her 30's.

FARAH: Aaron. There is this man I always see at the Beit Jala check-point. He's an old man. And every day he rides the bus, and everyday the soldiers make him get off the bus and he refuses! He yells at them, tells them they should treat him better. Yells at them they should respect him. Every day he does the same thing. And some days they beat him and some days they let him go and some days they just make him wait for hours. And every day he tries to teach them. Someone should make a movie about this man. You see how we live. No freedom to move about. It can take me hours to get to work in East Jerusalem. East Jerusalem! It's ten minutes from Ramallah. And I have the permissions. I have the papers. If you don't, forget it. You're not going anywhere.

When I lived abroad—I received my masters from Georgetown University—and I had my freedoms, could move about in peace, eat in peace, socialize in peace, I thought, how the hell did I ever live like *this?* Aaron, can you imagine? Watching on television, the bombing of your own people, 50 miles away? Watching children killed. People injured. *Missiles aimed at people!* It's vicious, these wars. So vicious. And there is nothing we can do. We are trapped here. Surrounded by this wall. Now, even if you protest, they arrest you.

Aaron, I am for peace. I work for the United Nations! And they are killing us. Some of my friends, trained in nonviolence. Worked in non-violent resistance for years.

Together with Israelis. Protesting. Legal actions. They are not for Hamas. But now they say, *no more.* They cut communication. *End the occupation.* They say. Then we will talk again. Some say it is time for armed resistance. I do not agree. I am for non-violence. No matter what. I studied the histories. I understand the cycles. Non-violence, for me, it is the air I breathe. It is who I am. But Aaron, we are only human beings. Can you blame them?

6.

Late night. Car ride back over the line. Bumpy road turned back smooth. Restricted way turned free-way. Israeli car. Israeli driver. Israeli license plate. No hassle. No checkpoint. No wait. Kalandia, a dusty dream. The other side of a line drawn in the sand. Watchtowers fade into night. Into East Jerusalem. Into West Jerusalem. Into my rented room. I lie awake in bed. Ceiling staring down at me. Headache.

Headlines:

Occupation; Invasion; Assassination;
Suicide Bombing; Bulldozing; Sbarros; Maxim; Jenin; Bil'in;
Temple Mount; Mount of Olives; Judea; Samarea;
Apartheid; Water Rights; Human Rights;
Hezbollah; Hamas; Fatah; Likud; Mossad; Shabbak;
'48; '67; '73; Refugee;
Golan; Iraq; Iran; Lebanon; Katushas; Qassams;
Homemade, Cluster, Roadside Bombs;
Ball Bearings, Nails, Shrapnel;
Milluim; Pigguim; M-16;
Kevlar; Tanks; Rocks; Sling Shots;
Mine Fields; Kidnapping; Tunnels; Terrorists;
Tel Aviv; Jerusalem; Jericho; Jordon; West Bank; Gaza Strip;
Boycott, Divestment, Sanction; Land appropriation;
Colonization; Two State Solution;
Settlement; Permanent; Right of Return;
Bomb Shelter; Peace Partner; Cease Fire; Cease Fire;
Hold Your Fire; *Sheket, Sheket!*

This trip to Israel is...

7.

My first trip to Israel was in 1993. I stepped off the plane at Ben Gurion airport and the sun blinded me. I walked down the rolling staircase, got on my knees and kissed the tarmac. The asphalt burned my lips. But I thought that's what you do when you arrive in the Holy Land.

The story of the Jewish people. Somehow I was a part of it. But I didn't really know *how* I was a part of it. My father's Yiddish Brooklyn was long gone. I felt outside of it. So there I was, dripping with sweat under the Middle Eastern sun and I needed to mark the moment. So I kissed the dirty ground. And all the other passengers rushed by me to get into the air-conditioned line at customs.

I took a bus to Jerusalem. There was a hostel there—they let you stay for free if you were there to study Torah. That's why I had come. Not for vacation. Not to tour the sites. I'd come to learn. I arrived at Jaffa Gate, the entrance to the Old City. The giant stone arch is a threshold.

Jerusalem.

I signed up for a Hebrew class. I wandered the narrow winding streets of the Jewish Quarter alone. There was something there. The light at night reflecting off the Jerusalem stone. I met an elder who taught a small class on Kabbalah. Around a table, early in the morning, we were parsing out a mystical Hebrew text. Word by word. Ideas nested inside ideas. Laughing. We made soup. It was the festival of *Sukkot*. We built a *sukkah* on the roof, and gazed at the stars through the palm leaves. We ate dates. And we talked about being Jews. About impermanence. About wandering in the desert. About home and homeland. And there I was. In Jerusalem. *Yerushalayim.* The ancient seat of Judaism. The modern capital of the Jewish nation. The very center of the Jewish story.

And I'm no longer looking in from the outside. I'm inside the story now.

> (sings)
> Shalom Aleichem,
> Malachey Hashareit
> Malachey, El Elyon...

We sing on Shabbat as the sun falls below Mt. Zion, welcoming the Sabbath bride, and her ministering angels.

Mi melech,
malchei hamlochim.

We smoke weed in the courtyards built of Jerusalem stone and study Torah.

Haka-a-dosh boruchu.

I feel like I've come home.

Hakadosh boruchu.

It was 1993. I was twenty five years old. It was a time when there was great hope from Oslo, and a final settlement between Israelis and Palestinians seemed just around the corner.

8.

This trip to Israel is...

ARIK: Aaron, my first session in Special Forces was between '76 and '80 and I spent most of it in Lebanon. All the terrorist organization was in Lebanon then. And there I was lucky to deal only with bad guys. Eh, because when you have, in Lebanon, you have a bad guy it's for sure it's a bad guy, this is an enemy, a terrorist, he should be killed. In 1990 I was, eh, commander in the territories, in the West Bank. In there *most* of the people are...innocent. Citizens. Population. Who is bad who is good? You can find yourself commanding 10 or 12 arrest missions in one night. So you take somebody out of his house in the middle of the night. He might be bad guy, he might be...just suspicious. Very light suspicious. Still, you take all the family, you take them outside, children, women. Should be done gently. You never...you never succeed in this.

It's problematic. So, you take the man out. If he is cooperating it goes quietly. If he's not you, eh, you destroy some of the house. And again it's for the good reason of protecting your soldier. I wouldn't send a soldier into a house while there is shooting from inside. So, let's bring a bulldozer and take the house. But the house is also the house of a least another twenty innocent wives, children, grandfather, grandmother— this is how a house in Tul Karim will look like. So you find yourself doing, maybe for the right purpose, or for your need, doing very bad things, very immoral things. Eh, the situation makes you.

Look, I was so many times in a position of thinking of, *seruv,* refusing. Refusing to serve. And I am a lieutenant commander, from Special Forces, it's not, eh... And I didn't. I didn't refuse and never even suggest to somebody else to refuse. I still don't think it's the right action to take. Why? Because, I see myself as somebody—I don't know if it's right to put it in English this way—with a high morality level. So it's better if I will be there than somebody else. If I'm not there, the position will be taken by somebody who doesn't give a shit about, eh, Palestinian every day life, etc.

The basic thing is: Are we in a war, or not? This is the question. If we are in a war, in a war you do lot of things which are immoral, not very nice. Eh, the Americans on the way to kill Saddam Hussein, they killed 60-70 thousand Iraqis—civilians—nobody gave a shit for this! I don't know, for me it's a little too much even for a war. Here, the IDF try to warn civilians. Dropping papers, phone calls, eh, *get out of your houses,* etc. *Try.* If it's a war, I really believe the Israeli

IDF is...eh, in quite a high morality level. If you *don't* take it as a war, we are doing harmful, bad things. Okay?

It's difficult. We must destroy the tunnels. They're a threat to our security. To our life. So we destroy them. And they send rockets from a school. A school! Using children as shields. What you expect we do? It's a difficult situation. Is it a war? What they say in Israel is the terrorist organization force us, for a kind of a war. It's still a war, but it's very different because it's from civilian areas. And it never ends. It just goes on and on and on.

9.

JACOB: Aaron, it's not fair the way Israel is criticized by the outside world, it's just not right. But when it comes from the inside, when *Jews* criticize Israel, it drives me fucking crazy! Yes, Israel's done some things I don't agree with. But I'm gonna contribute to the lynch mob out there by saying so publicly?! Ha! You have to understand something, in this part of the world they see *self-criticism as weakness*. Do you see Jordan criticizing itself? No. Do you see Saudi Arabia debating its human rights violations in the press? Fuck No. Why? Because their press is run by the State. Okay?!

Let me tell you something. I'm proud of the free democratic society we've built here in the Middle East. I'm proud that we've got Palestinians elected to the *Knesset.* Tell me, what Arab country has Jews in its parliament? I'm proud of women's rights in Israel. I'm proud that the gays in Jerusalem are protected. I'm proud of that. In Cairo, they beat 'em up and throw 'em in Jail. And we're the bad guys?! I'm so sick and tired of this god-damn double-standard! Israel is always on trial. After sixty years of statehood, we still have to justify ourselves to the rest of the world. More than sixty years! And we're still talking about our *right to exist?!*

I got news for you: statehood ain't pretty. It's called real-politik, kid. Look over your notes from Poli Sci 101. I'm not just being a right-wing hard-ass, Aaron. I'm not. I'm a Democrat for god's sake. I'm being realistic. Take Iran: Keep them from getting the bomb. Whatever it takes. I mean what*ever* it takes. What the hell are we waiting for? Some people think Jews have some higher moral obligation. Why? Why?! It's us or them. That's how it is. *Us* or *them.* That's how it's been the whole time. They don't want us here. It's sad. But it's true. We're talking about our survival. That's what we're talking about. And to survive in this neighborhood you need power. So what we're really talking about is Jewish power. Look at history: Jewish survival; Jewish power. And some people are uncomfortable with Jewish power. I'm not, Aaron. Jewish power was hard won. And we will keep it.

10.

TALI: Aaron, it's our job to be critical of human rights abuses, no matter who commits them. B'Tselem is an human rights organization. I met with the Generals. Me. And the Generals, right? And they say to me "B'Tselem is hurting us in our war against terrorism." And I say, "Wait a minute, wait a minute! — there's the metaphor of the war, right? The *propaganda* war, we are hurting you in the propaganda war. Maybe," I say, "maybe we are hurting you in the propaganda war. But the actual war," these are Generals, "the *actual* war in Gaza, how are we hurting you?" Because there *is* a war of information, Aaron, but nobody is *dying* in the war of information. But the Generals say to me, "No, no, you *are* hurting us. Because if the British government will not sell us replacement parts for our tanks, because of B'Tselem's publication of human rights violations, that threatens our security."

But Aaron! We don't want Israel to be just a military fortress, do we?! So I say to the Generals, "Look, the fact that we are Israelis criticizing our own government, defending Palestinian human rights, that's the *best* face of Israel. *We* are the sort of public-relations *dream* of the Foreign Ministry--show the world: look at what a great democracy we are!"

11.

PROF. HOROWITZ: We believe in a whole number of things on the Left, don't we, Aaron? Equality, democracy, equity for lesbians and gays and for women and for, you know, the rule of law, and we're against fascism, against totalitarianism and so on. And some people take one element, anti-imperialism for example, and raise it, to a kind of *principle.* And this one principle becomes a kind of guiding rule. And there are lots of very very intelligent people who do this. And it leads them into all sorts of very strange places.

This *guiding principle* leads a lot of people, for example, to support Hamas, on the basis that they are the most militantly anti-imperialist Palestinians. And so from a principle of opposing imperialism they have come to a place where they support an organization that is similar to a fascistic organization. And it leads some serious people to move to recognize *Hezballah* as part of the global Left, which is astonishing. Because there's nothing Left about them. Nothing. I don't know, one could call them clerical fascists—I don't think I would. But, you know, we know what they're for: they're for smashing the labor movement, they're against lesbian and gay rights, they're against women's rights, they're for a theocratic state and they're for killing Jews. Excuse me, but I don't see how that's part of the global Left!

There's an old Bundist joke from the 20's: what's the definition of a Zionist? Do you know this one, Aaron? A Zionist is one Jew who gives money to a second Jew so that a third Jew can go live in Palestine. *(laughs)* It was a *lunatic,* utopian minority, idiotic political project. You know, let's leave Vienna, or leave Berlin, or leave Lodj, and go and build something in a marshland in the Middle East, where there are people are already living. It was madness, actually. And it was never going to work. Never mind the pogroms. And what made it real...was the Holocaust. What, if you like, as a Marxist, what transformed the material condition, what transformed it from an idea into a reality was the Holocaust. Was a kind of wholesale change of the condition of Jewish life in Europe. And it's not a justification. I'm not waving the shroud of Auschwitz in order to defend breaking the arms of Palestinians, I'm just saying that something changed in Europe that transformed Zionism from a rather silly idea, into a state. And with hindsight, of course, it looks a bit less silly than it did at the time.

12.

DR. TZIPORA: We are at war with biology, Aaron. We are so deep inside a repeating cycle of trauma. It's physiological. We are social primates. We crave contact; intimacy; warmth; love. We are biologically dependent on social connection. We have nerves, here, around the eyes. The vegal nerves. For social cueing. 90 percent of communication is without words! From the time we are born. I am an infant. Held at mother's breast. I can see only 7 inches. What do I see? Mother's eyes. She gazes at her new baby. I am seen. I am acknowledged. This is where I begin to receive the social cueing that will support my life. That tells me I am safe. I am cared for. I am loved.

Now. What happens when mother is living in a war? Under immense stress. She hold me to her breast. But she turn her eyes. Mother is tense. Father is away at war. Perhaps father has been killed. Perhaps father return from battle and is rough with mother. Home is filled with stress. Mother is nervous. Mother is afraid. I am a tiny baby. I pick up on these cues. No words have to pass. The cuing happens here. *(The eyes).* From the first days of my life, the message is clear: Mother is not safe. I am not safe. We see it here in the clinic every day. Grown men and women. In the eyes: *I am not safe.* I have experienced it on the street myself!

Now, look at Israel. 1948. Refuges coming from Europe, after the cataclysm of the Holocaust. They do not speak of it. They hold the trauma inside. They never release it! They don't know how. What they know from Post Traumatic Stress Disorder? Now, imagine raising a child. Holding that child to your breast. With Holocaust trauma in your head. In your body. What that child see in your eyes? Horror. Fear. Mistrust. Passed on in the first weeks of the child's life. Then the child grow. Every few years, war. More trauma. Then the child go to the army. Then they raise their child. Generation to generation. And the trauma is never released!

1948. Palestinians suffer trauma. Expulsion from their homes. The killing in that war. Aaron! I do not compare *levels* of trauma. It is irrelevant. Trauma is trauma. You think a baby care if you are Israeli or Palestinian? *Tsk.* The message in the eyes is the same: I am not safe. This is not politics, Aaron. It is physiology. Now, look at Palestinians living in refugee camps for three generations. What you think is happening there? Recycled trauma. The message: *I am not safe.* It is an infected wound, a dis-ease, carried in the body.

We are two societies living in profound fear. And to end it, we must have trust. We must know with our eyes, not words, that we are safe. We must discharge these built up feelings of anger and hurt. They must be released.

Aaron Davidman in performance at Intersection for the Arts,
San Francisco, March 2014. Photo by Ken Friedman.

Intersection for the Arts, San Francisco, March 2014. Photos by Allen Willner.

Intersection for the Arts, San Francisco, March 2014. Photo by Ken Friedman.

Intersection for the Arts, March 2014. Photo by Ken Friedman.

PlayMakers Rep, Chapel Hill, January 2015. Photo by Wolfgang Wachalovsky.

Marines' Memorial Theatre, San Francisco, Oct. 2015. Photo by Tom Kubik.

Marines' Memorial Theatre, San Francisco, Oct. 2015. Photo by Tom Kubik.

13.

I'm in the Palestinian village of Carawat Bin Zaid in the West Bank. I'm here with a group of activists: Palestinian and Jewish Israeli women who've come to support the Palestinian women of this village. They're a lively group. I had a difficult time finding our meeting place in Haifa, and when I finally showed up one of the women said, "Come on! We've never waited this long for a man before!"

Tamar Gozansky is with us. She used to be a member of the Knesset. I sat next to her on the ride here.

> TAMAR: The situation is completely about the occupation. Israel has been an occupying force for nearly 50 years. Only from 1948 to 1967 was Israel not engaged in the occupation of the territories. An entire generation has grown up in this occupation—on both sides—and it's all they know. Yes, Israel is a democratic nation because it holds open elections. But more than 2 million Palestinians live in the West Bank under the control of the government of Israel. And they do not have a vote. You cannot have a true democracy without voting rights. Without human rights. Historically, Jews all over the world were pioneers in the fight for human rights. I'm proud of this. It helps define who I am as a Jew. But it's not the case in Israel.

Carawat Bin Zaid is a small village built into a hillside. Cinderblock homes, dusty roads, unfinished buildings. We're in a modest house that looks out over the town. Nadia is the leader of our group. A Palestinian citizen of Israel and lifetime activist, she's an elegant older woman. She introduces me to our hosts. From a large bay window I see the dirt road we drove in on in the valley below. There are framed photographs on the wall of four boys and a woman. There's Arabic writing around the pictures. I ask Nadia about the woman.

NADIA: Yasmina Jabar. She was killed. By Israeli sniper.
AARON : I don't understand.
NADIA: Look, in the hills there, they say. Two weeks ago. IDF. Army sniper. She has husband and seven children. What they will do?
AARON: IDF sniper?
NADIA: It's why we have come today, Aaron. To pay respect. To show the women of this village, they are not alone.

I turn to one of the Jewish women in our group.

AARON: Does the IDF do this?

She gives me a look.

WOMAN: *(gestures, what do you think?!)*

There's activity in the street below. An IDF armored jeep is coming into town.

NADIA: Look, look at the children running. Look at their excitement. They think it is a game!

A woman is yelling at her kid to get back inside, but he runs off. It's a sudden swarm from all ends of the village as young men and boys are running towards the jeep, not away from it. Two guys on a rooftop are gathering pieces of cinder block to throw. Boys are picking up rocks.

NADIA: Get away from the window. The soldiers may shoot. Come! It is not safe.

We back away. The jeep passes through the village and disappears around the hill. The boys drop their rocks. The young men disperse and go on their way.

27

We're called to eat. An enormous feast has been prepared. Large flat bread soaked in olive oil and baked with ground lamb, sautéed onion and spices. Roasted chicken. Soup. Chopped tomato and cucumber salad. Fresh yogurt. All cooked out back in an underground oven and over an open fire. It's one of the most delicious meals I have ever had in my life.

NADIA: Aaron, I want you to meet Ma'moon.

I shake Ma'moon's hand. He's about fourteen. His clothes are a little dirty. His body slumps to one side. He looks like he's in pain.

NADIA: The soldiers were taunting the boys. Yelling names about their mothers. About their sisters. This kind of thing. And the boys start to throw rocks. And the soldiers start to shoot. And Ma'moon is shot in the back. And his intestines do not work.

Ma'moon wears a New York Yankees cap. He forces a smile for me. We try to communicate. There's something missing in his eyes. He's lost. This kid. Completely lost.

NADIA: I am trying to raise money and make arrangement for him to have surgery in Haifa. We will see.

The meal is finished. Ma'moom hasn't eaten a thing.

Next, on to the main event: an outdoor assembly in a large schoolyard. There are several hundred people, mostly women wearing head scarves, seated in rows of chairs facing a stage. There are decorations celebrating traditional Palestinian women: embroidered dresses, pottery, a flour grinder. Girls are holding banners. They seat us in front, like a row of dignitaries. There are speeches. They're giving out a hundred certificates to honor women volunteering for health and agriculture programs.

> NADIA: Aaron, we are trying to give this village an alternative to Hamas. Many of these girls are married so young. Fourteen, fifteen years old. And they stop going to school. We must give them education. We must teach them.

A young girl comes on stage and sings a beautiful song. Then several older girls come on in traditional dress. They're smiling and dancing for the crowd.

> *(Dances)*

14.

I'm on the street. Hebron, West Bank. I'm here to meet Nabil, a Palestinian field worker for B'Tselem. A crowd is gathered around a man in the back of a pickup truck. He shouts into a megaphone. His Arabic is harsh. The crowd is animated. Some kind of demonstration. I listen for "Yahudi", the Arabic word for Jew. Am I in the right place? The sun is hot. I step into a shadow. Nabil is late. The man with the megaphone thrusts his fist into the air. The crowd responds. I can feel the tension. I took a taxi from Bethlehem. Dropped in the middle of Hebron. I don't really know where the hell I am. The man on the megaphone gets louder. The crowd is shouting back. A man with dark eyes is watching me. Fuck.

> NABIL: Aaron? Forgive me, I am late. You are welcome.
> AARON: Thank you.
> NABIL: I am pleased to meet you.
> AARON: Pleased to meet you Nabil.
> NABIL: You're journey, it was good?
> AARON: It was fine. Can we go?
> NABIL: Is everything alright? You look frightened.
> AARON: This crowd...

NABIL: This?
AARON: What is it?
NABIL : An auction.
(beat)
NABIL: You want a television?
AARON : No. I don't want a television.
NABIL: Come. I will give you a tour of Hebron.

We walk through the narrow stone streets of the Old City of Hebron. The tomb of Abraham and Sarah is said to be here. Religious Jews and Muslims pray at this tomb every day. In separate, heavily guarded areas. We sit at a small plastic table and drink coffee with Nabil's friend who owns a shop near the tomb. I think I insult him when I offer to pay for my drink.

Out of nowhere, four Israeli soldiers emerge from the narrow maze in full battle gear. Flack jackets, helmets, automatic weapons. Their faces are so young. Shoulders at their ears. Guns pressed to their chests. Eyes shifting. One kid makes eye contact with me for a moment. A spilt second, as they pass. He looks confused. As if he recognizes me to say, *what are you doing here?* And I feel confused. Who is the stranger in this moment? I'm the outsider, the foreigner. *I* am the stranger. The Palestinians and Israelis live together, know each other so well. But the *soldier* is the stranger, as the Palestinian men and I sit together and watch him pass. But *Nabil* is the stranger, because I know these boys. These are our boys. Our sweet Jewish boys. They look like my counselors from summer camp. But they're so armored-up. And so vulnerable. The shifting points-of-view rip through that moment so fast.
Nabil is not phased by the soldiers.

NABIL: Come, Aaron. There is an American staying with me. I want you to meet him.

15.

Nabil's house sits on the side of a hill overlooking a
beautiful valley. It's dusk. From his patio I see farms and
fields, and lights on in the village below.

> NABIL: Fa'wahr. Refugee camp. I was raised there.
> With my brothers and my sisters. Hamas is there now.
> More and more Hamas. It is a problem. These religious.
> Big problem. Hamas. "Devotion and zeal in the path of
> Allah."

We stay up late drinking Turkish coffee and smoking
cigarettes with Daniel, an American medical student
staying with Nabil. He's volunteering at a hospital in
Hebron for the semester. He marches each week with the
protesters in the village of Bil'in.

> DANIEL: Hamas is the lesser of two evils!
> AARON: Hamas is a gang of fascist zealots!
> DANIEL: Aaron, Fatah is on the payroll of the United
> States!
> AARON: Fatah is the rule of law in the West Bank!
> DANEIL: They can't be trusted!
> AARON: You can trust Hamas?
> DANIEL: They were *elected!*
> AARON: So was your senator, but you don't seem to
> trust him.
> DANIEL: He's complicit with an Apartheid
> government.
> AARON: Can you stay on one topic for more than five
> seconds? You gotta go to Apartheid?
> DANIEL: Sue me.
> AARON: Hamas took control of Gaza by murdering
> Fatah leaders.
> DANIEL: Fatah wasn't giving up control!
> AARON: They threw them off of buildings for God's
> sake. These people are barbarians.

DANIEL: They were *elected*. I'm not saying they're saints, but welcome to statehood. You can't ask for democracy and then reject the leaders that the people voted for!

AARON: The people voted for Shariah law?

DANIEL: They voted for bread! Hamas is feeding them. While Fatah sit on their asses in Ramallah, cooperating with the Israelis who have ALL THE POWER.

AARON: What about the fact that--

DANIEL: Suicide bombers.

AARON: What?

DANIEL: You're going to bring up suicide bombers.

AARON: How do you know what I'm going to—

DANIEL: I can read you like a playbook for the American Jew.

AARON: *You're* an American Jew!

DANIEL: Do you really think a suicide bomber is any worse than the Israeli Air Force dropping a ten ton bomb on an apartment building to kill one man? If you're in that building, you're lucky if you're dead. You know how many children have been maimed because of the fucking Israelis and their "elected officials." And you call the Palestinians the terrorists?!

AARON: I haven't called *anyone* a terrorist!

DANIEL: Suicide bomber. Whatever.

AARON: You have to deal with security. You have to. The Israelis have been killed and maimed too. I was in Tel Aviv when a bus bomb—

DANIEL: Have you ever been to Gaza?

AARON: Stop changing the subject!

DANIEL: I'm not for bombing buses! But it's nothing compared to how Israel has ravaged Gaza. It's a *siege!* Horrible medical services, malnutrition—

AARON: You don't have to lecture me about Gaza.

DANIEL: It's one of the most densely populated places on the planet.

AARON: I know. So let's support agriculture. Let's support sustainability. Then maybe they'll stop sending missiles into S'derot.

DANIEL: They're sending missiles into S'derot because they *have* no agriculture! They have no sustainability. Israel's cut supply lines, closed borders, closed ports, closed fishing. They're starving in there! Their life is shit.

AARON: I thought Hamas was feeding them.

DANIEL: You know what I mean.

AARON: They're starving because Hamas spends all their money on tunnels and weapons *instead* of feeding people. They are a theocracy Daniel! They're trying rebuild the Caliphate of the entire Middle East.

DANIEL: Well, Hamas was nothing for decades, you know. A fringe radical group supported by Israel to destabilize Arafat. Now they have power and Israel can't control them. Who's fault is that?!

AARON: Iran sends them weapons!

DANIEL: I'm not saying I support violence. But they have a right to fight for themselves. You would say the Israelis have a right to defend themselves.

AARON: Of course.

DANIEL: The Palestinians are defending themselves.

AARON: Then you do support violence!

DANIEL: Self defense!

AARON: What do your parents think you're doing here?

DANIEL: Now who's changing the subject?

AARON: --

DANIEL: Hamas is the lesser of two evils. That's all I said.

AARON: The Hamas charter openly calls for the death of all Jews.

DANIEL: Scour the internet, you can find whatever you want. That charter is outdated. They want freedom.

AARON: Bullshit Daniel! Words mean something! They openly call for the destruction of a sovereign state and for the death of *all Jews*. You're a Jew! Doesn't that bother you?

DANIEL: Enough with the Jew stuff! I'm a Jew. So what? I'm also a human being. And here, I'm sorry, that trumps bagels and lox and Chanukah! What the fuck do you want from me, Aaron? I'm post-tribal. I'm post-religious. In fact, you could say, I'm *very* Jewish. I'm a revolutionary! Moses would be proud.
AARON: Oh PLEASE!
DANIEL: What?! I'm fighting for the under-dog. Remember the Holocaust? Apparently not!
AARON: Now who's reading from the playbook?! The holocaust survivors have become the perpetrators!
DANIEL: I didn't say that!
AARON: You did say it!
DANIEL: Didn't!
AARON: Did.
DANIEL: Didn't.
AARON: Did.
DANIEL: Didn't.
AARON: Did.
DANIEL: Didn't.
AARON: THERE ARE NO GAS CHAMBERS IN ISRAEL. STOP. JUST STOP.
DANIEL: WHO SAID ANYTHING ABOUT GAS CHAMBERS?! WE'RE TALKING ABOUT THE OCCUPATION AND SUBJUGATION OF ANOTHER PEOPLE FOR 5O YEARS!

(Silence)

I leave in the morning. Nabil takes me for breakfast and drives me to the bus.

NABIL: Thank you for coming Aaron. For seeing how we live.
AARON: Thank you for breakfast Nabil.
NABIL: It is not easy, Aaron. For any of us.

I take the bus back to Jerusalem.

That argument. It sticks to me like a nasty sore. My stomach is in knots. I'm furious with myself for losing my cool. Before Hebron, I was sure there was something whole that had broken, that needed to be put back together. But I can't piece *anything* together here. The pieces don't fit together. And then it occurs to me, on the bus, that maybe...maybe the fragments are all we have.

16.

AVRAM: There is a reason we are called Jews. We are descendants of the Kingdom of Judah. There is power in names, Aaron.

Aharon. Nachon? Atah ha Kohen? You could be a *Kohen,* you know this? It is a very big honor to be a descendent of the high-priests. *(He raises his hand in the Vulcan salute).* You think Star Trek invented this? Let me tell you, (*He raises his arms into the Kohanim priestly gesture)* God was going where no man had gone before...long before Spock and Captain Kirk.

Judea and Samaria was promised. It is meant for Jews. The settlement of the land of Israel is a commandment of God. Our exile is over. We were running for two thousand years. We're not running any more. We've come home. East Jerusalem/West Jerusalem, tsk— There is only...*Jerusalem*. The undivided capitol of Israel. *Baruch Atah Hashem, bonay Yerushalayim. Blessed are You, God, Builder of Jerusalem.* It is our birthright to be here in this land. From the Jordan River to the Mediterranean Sea. It's a tiny sliver of land in such a big world. Is it so much to ask to be left alone?

Yes. There is power in names. *Palestine* is a name. *Palestine* is a name given to this land in an attempt to wipe out Jewish history. You think I am politically incorrect to say such a thing. Or perhaps you know I am talking about the Romans in the Second Century.

When they conquered Jerusalem they changed the name of this region from "Principia Judea" to "Syria Palaestina." *Palestine.* The Romans wanted to be done with us. It wasn't enough that they slaughtered our people and destroyed our temple. No. They wanted to erase our name from history. And, literally, wipe us off the map. Well...we're back. To reclaim our land. And to defend it from our enemies.

Aharon, I know why you are here. You are here to prove to us that our settlements are wrong. And that you are right. You have drunk the cool-aide of *Galut*—the Jews of the Diaspora. And you see us living in the land of our Fathers as isolationist and we are a threat to your liberal view of Judaism.

Forgive me, *Aharon,* but your Judaism does not interest me. *You* interest me, *Aharon.* You interest me for one reason: your *neshama.* You know what means *neshama?* Your soul. The Jewish soul is a very special soul that is put here on this earth for a very specific reason. I wish you would come live here with us *Aharon.* I will never impress you with my speech. But this place. This land. *Yerushalayim. Chevron. Beit Lechem.* These places are filled with light. They are holy places. This land will impress you. It will open your heart. We have a job to do *Aharon.* To repair this broken world. And we must do it here. The outside world will never understand us. *Amelek* will never understand us. Stop trying to please the world, *Aharon.* We have already the impossible task of pleasing God.

If you think peace will come to Israel only when we give back land to the Arabs, I say to you, show me the proof. Show me the example. You can't. Because there isn't one. We gave Sinai back to Egypt. An embarrassment of weakness. But it was done. And look at Egypt now. The withdrawal from Gaza? We gave the land. Tell me, where is the peace? I see only Hamas, determined, *determined,* like the Romans, to wipe us off the map. And you want me to give them the keys to *Jerusalem? Jerusalem?!* The seat of the throne of God? The heart of the world? They will slaughter us.

17.

IBRAHIM: The only Israelis I have known wear uniforms. The only Israelis I have known carry guns. The only Israelis I have known decide where I can live, where I can travel, when I can travel. The only Israelis my children have known drive tanks, invade neighborhoods, intimidate their parents at check points. The only Israelis I have known own the water trucks that deliver my water! My water!!

It's not balanced. There is the occupier and there is the occupied. And what can we do? My family's orchard was our life for five generations. Yes, three hundred years, for sure, three hundred, probably more. Many more. And now my orchard is destroyed. They say for security. For this Wall.

Let me tell you something, Aaron. Please do not be upset. The Holocaust was not my fault. You understand what I say? I am sorry for the Jewish. But my grandfather was not Hitler. He was farmer here, in Palestine. Three thousand kilometers away. And when the Jewish come, he would not sell them land. He would not. But he watched. He watched them coming. And now I watch, I watch them coming. And I watch them building. On my grandfather's land. On my land. And they are more Israelis for me to "know."

There will be no two state solution. There will be one country here in Palestine. Islam ruled *Al Quds,*

Jerusalem, for more than one thousand years before the Jewish. The Jewish have been here some sixty years. We are a patient people. We will wait. Population is the best weapon. Aaron, You must not worry. The Jewish will be fine. They will be cared for. Allah is merciful. Allah loves the Jewish. They were his first people. But we will rule this land again.

18.

RABBI MOSES: This is not my Judaism. I've been a rabbi for thirty years, Aaron. I've been coming to Israel since before the Six Day War. I have family here. This is not my Judaism. The State of Israel is not my *Judaism*.

Sh'ma Yisrael Adonai Elohainu Adonai Echad.
I say it every day. This, the *Sh'ma*, is arguably the most important text in all of Judaism. It's so important, not only am I commanded to say it every day, not only do I wrap myself physically with this prayer—a scroll inside my *t'fillin*,—but I am commanded to say it when I die. I am commanded to say these words, if possible, with my last breath. What is so very important about this one sentence that I should say it every day of my life, wrap my body in it and spend my last breath on it?

Sh'ma Yisrael Adonai Elohainu Adonai Echad.

Sh'ma. Hear. Listen. *Yisrael.* Israel. Listen People of Israel. *Adonai Elohainu.* God, *our* God. *Adonai Echad.* God is One. Now, whatever your God is or isn't. Whatever you believe or don't believe, Aaron, it's these last two words that are important: *Adonai Echad.* What does it mean? Perhaps the most misunderstood two words in all of Western Civilization! *Adonai Echad* does NOT mean there is only one God. *Adonai Echad* means God is One. What's the difference? There's a HUGE difference. God is One. *One,* not the number.

One, the truth of indivisibility. Wholeness. *Adonai Echad.*

These two words are Judaism's greatest gift to the world. Abraham is living in a time of human sacrifice, and here comes the idea that God is not out there in the heavens, apart from us. But God is all things, including us! God is the interconnectedness of all of life on this earth and all that's out there in the stars. It's the Big Bang, Quantum Theory, String Theory, the *Tao,* the Buddha, Love, call it what you want. We're all interconnected. That's the message. That's the Jewish message. *Adonai Echad.* We are God. Yes. *We* are God. *Sh'ma Yisrael Adonai Elohainu Adonai Echad.* Listen, Israel, God, Our God, God is One. Indivisible. There is no *Other.* It's time to end human sacrifice. That was the radical message. Three thousand years ago!

And we're still killing each other. We're still sacrificing our children. We still claim God as "our God," ownable, knowable. *We know what God wants.*

We don't know shit.

Adonai Echad. We say it every day: *Listen, Israel. We are all connected.* Stop the killing. Stop the killing!

This is not my Judaism.

But what about THEM? They'll say. This is the Middle East. We have to protect ourselves. This is the way the world is.

Aaron, Judaism is my religion. In this religion we worship Yud Hay Vav Hay. The Hebrew letters of God's name. Yud Hay Vav Hay is not the God of *what is.* Yud Hay Vav Hay is the God of what *ought to be.* The God of *Becoming.* The God of *Possibility.* The creative force of transformation. *Why do so many people throughout history hate the Jews?!* They ask me. Because we DON'T accept the world *the way it is.* Because, as Rabbi Heschel taught us, the greatest sin in this life is the sin of despair. Because our heritage is a heritage of shit-stirring. Because we revolted against our captivity in Egypt. We broke the circle of slavery: Moses. We broke the circle of human sacrifice: Abraham. We broke the confinement of the dark ages into the Enlightenment: Spinoza. We broke the class system in Russia: Trotsky. We helped break the race barrier in the United States. We drained the swamps in *Erez Yisrael* and built an amazing country here in the Middle East! We are inventors. We are creators. We are storytellers. We are agents of change. We are light unto the nations. Light!

This is my Judaism.

My Judaism is NOT a Judaism of expulsion and land grabs; My Judaism is not a Judaism of concrete walls and settlements; My Judaism is not a Judaism of cluster bombs and armored bulldozers; My Judaism does not bomb UN shelters; My Judaism is not a Judaism of massacre.

My Judaism sees the sanctity of all life. My Judaism calls for compassion and generosity. My Judaism builds bridges not walls. My Judaism says *Sh'ma! Sh'ma Yisrael, Adonai Elohainu, Adonai Echad.*

19.

AMIR: Aaron. *Aharon.* You come all the way to the Dead Sea from America. Pshhhhh. American. I would like to live in America. You are lucky. American. But your music is shit. Your pop music. You like trance? It's deep. You can lose yourself inside it.

(Amir takes a hit from a joint.)

It's a far way. To travel here. To this remote place. On a dry hillside. Look at it. The Dead Sea. *Yam Hamélach.*

I like it here. Open space. Too much noise in *Yerushalayim.* It's too intense. The air here. I can breathe. I take long walks in these hills. Sometimes I can imagine, from just up here, when I look out over the Sea, to the other side. To Jordan. I can just imagine *Moshe*—Moses—there. With his flock. Looking out to this land, this Promised Land, he would not ever put his foot inside. With his staff in the air...*(laughs)*...It's crazy. To me. The Bible. And all the people so angry. It really happened! It did it not! Who cares? It's a story. You know? A wisdom story. But this land, these hills, they feel like something...like spirits are here, yeah? I sound strange. Well. I'm healing. Healing.

(He hits the joint.)

I used to read the paper. To follow politics. I don't even watch TV anymore. I don't listen to the news. It's...I cannot. I have only to work in the kitchen. I am a dishwasher. And read my books. And listen to music. You like Bob Dylan?! Wow. Okay. *One* American. He's deep. My girlfriend *loved* Bob Dylan.

I don't have a girlfriend now. I have nightmares. So...it's not so easy. To be with me. To sleep by my side. I have to...find my way first. Then, some day. I've had therapy. Lots of therapy. I only lasted six months in the army. Six months. After that I thought I would go to India. All my friends go to India after the army. I thought I would go to "find myself." But then I thought...if I can't find myself here, how I am going to find myself in India?

(Laughs. He goes inward.)

It was on Ben Yehuda Street. In high school. With my friends. And...you know what means *piggua?* ...A bomber...exploded himself. And because I happened to be...standing at a corner...protected by a wall...I am here. I...exist. But my two friends...

You know, in Torah, in the Bible, there are 3 commandments to love. You know this? Only 3, in the whole Bible. Love who? Love God. *V'ahavta et Adonai.* Okay. That one is obvious. Don't have to believe in God, by the way, just love God. What's Number 2? Love your neighbor as yourself. *V'ahavta l'rayachah Kamocha.* No surprise there. May be difficult for some...but....What's the third? Love your parents? No. Love your wife, your husband? No. Your children? No. The Stranger. *V'ahavtem et haGer.*

We are commanded, *commanded*, to *Love the Stranger.*

(Song/beats)

20.

A few days later, I enter the Old City of Jerusalem at Jaffa Gate. The sun is setting. Shop keepers are closing up. I wander through the narrow winding streets. Here I am again. In this ancient place. The stones beneath my feet worn smooth by millions of pilgrims over the centuries.

And I when I get to the wide open plaza at the *Kotel,* the Western Wall, I take a *kipa* from the bin and cover my head as is custom. And standing before this massive wall I remember that Jews wear a *kipa* not only to pay respect to that which is above us, but to mark the place where we end and the rest of the world begins. To mark the edge between the small temple of my body and the vastness of everything else.

And staring up at this towering ancient wall I feel the right size in relation to the universe. Like standing at the edge of the ocean or under the stars on a clear night—it's a relief to feel so small.

I close my eyes.
I see into the past
I look into the future
And I am alone
And I have wrestled with God's angel all night
And she says
Let me go for the day has broken
And I say
Not until you bless me
And she says
What is your name?
And I say
Aaron. My name is Aaron.
And she says
You are Israel
Yisrael
For you have struggled with God and with men

And I cling to the stone. Press my lips to the wall with a kiss. I feel the cool rock against my face. I open my eyes...and I'm staring at little pieces of paper crammed into the cracks and crevices of the wall. Little bits of prayer and wishes and dreams of people from all over the world. *Please.* You can hear the cry inside the cracks. *Please, God, help me. Help us.* The Wailing Wall holds the tears of generations.

And I cannot contain the fragments; the sparks I've pulled from behind the eyes of every single person I've met. They smash up against each other. And I'm bursting. I'm exploding into a million shards.

(sings)
Sh'ma Yisrael
Sh'ma Yisrael

Sh'ma
Adonai Elohainu
Adonai Echad

And as the muezzin's call-to-prayer
floats out over the Wall
from the Al-Aqsa mosque above
I return my kipa into the bin,
tip my head toward the *Kotel*
and wander back
through the narrow winding streets
of the Old City of Jerusalem.
Al Quds. The Holy.
Yeru-shalayim. City of Peace.

(sings)
Sh'ma Yisrael
Sh'ma Yisrael
Sh'ma
Adonai Elohainu
Adonai Echad
Echad
Echad
Echad

END

ACKNOWLEGEMENTS

The premiere production was funded in part by the Walter and Elise Haas Fund, the Jewish Community Federation & Endowment Fund, the Zellerbach Family Foundation and many individual contributors. My sincere gratitude to these foundations and to each and every contributor.

This play was written to be a solo performance, but by no means is it a solo project. A multitude of people and organizations helped make this text possible. Thank you to: my collaborator and director Michael John Garcés; Sara Schwartz Geller, Corey Fischer, Naomi Newman and Traveling Jewish Theatre; Ari Roth and Theatre J; Philip Himberg and Sundance Institute Theatre Program; Randy Rollison and Intersection for the Arts; Cornerstone Theater Company; Stephanie Rapp; Daniel Sokatch; Sydney Mintz; Marcus Gardley; Justine Shapiro; David Katznelson; Aaron Posner; Becky Buckwald, Orli Bein and the New Israel Fund San Francisco office; Dan Cohn; Lisa Erdberg; Hannah Kranzberg; Amy Mueller and Playwrights Foundation; Georges Lammam; Danny Maseng; Meirav Kupperberg; Ibrahim Miari; Jessica Montell; Ati Citron; David Hirsh; Scot Nichols; Dena Martinez; Deb Fink; Larry Davidman; Naomi Davidman; on tour, Wolfgang Wachalovsky; in life, my daughter Zoe; in love, Sarana; and finally, and most importantly, gratitude to the good people of Israel and Palestine who invited me into their homes and told me their stories.

Peace, Salaam, Shalom.

–Aaron

ABOUT THE AUTHOR

Aaron Davidman is a playwright, actor and director. He is drawn to stories of ethnic history and cultural complexity that challenge our assumptions of the "other." Aaron served as Artistic Director of Traveling Jewish Theatre in San Francisco from 2002-2011. He received his theatrical training at Carnegie Mellon University, earned a BA from the University of Michigan and an MFA in creative writing/playwriting from San Francisco State University.

More at **aarondavidman.com**.

ABOUT THE PROJECT

WRESTLING JERUSALEM is a play (directed by Michael John Garcés) and a feature film (directed by Dylan Kussman) that seeks to build bridges of understanding in communities torn by polemic. Post-performance and post-screening conversations give audiences an opportunity to reflect, as a community, on the issues that the work brings forward. If you are interested in bringing the performance or a screening of the film to your community, place of worship or school, please contact:

info@wrestlingjerusalem.com

More information about the play and the film:
wrestlingjerusalem.com

Made in the USA
San Bernardino, CA
07 March 2019